CRACKING
THE
CODE
TO A SUCCESSFUL
INTERVIEW

D1290357

CRACKING
THE
CODE
TO A SUCCESSFUL
INTERVIEW

15 Insider Secrets from a Top-Level Recruiter

EVAN PELLETT

POQUOSON PUBLIC LIBRARY
500 CITY HALL AVENUE
POQUOSON, VA 23662

BLACKSTONE
PUBLISHING

Copyright © 2016 by Evan Pellett
Published in 2016 by Blackstone Publishing
Edited by Karen Ford
Jacket and interior design by Kathryn Galloway English

All rights reserved. This book or any portion thereof
may not be reproduced or used in any manner whatsoever
without the express written permission of the publisher
except for the use of brief quotations in a book review.

Printed in the United States of America

First edition: 2016
ISBN 978-1-4417-0053-7

1 3 5 7 9 10 8 6 4 2

CIP data for this book is available
from the Library of Congress

Blackstone Publishing
31 Mistletoe Rd.
Ashland, OR 97520

www.BlackstonePublishing.com

*Dedicated to anyone who has glimpsed
a doorway to new horizons but saw no
pathway to get there; to those who provide
the key and shine a light on the path; and to
my wonderful parents, Karin and George.*

TABLE OF CONTENTS

FOREWORD

I'm going to guess that you consider yourself bright, motivated, and articulate. You might be just out of school and at the beginning of a job search. Maybe you're going for an internal promotion, or for a first or second interview. You could even be a seasoned executive or worker. No matter where you are in your career, one universal concept is absolutely critical if you're going to get to the next step: the interview is the key to success at all levels.

In the course of this book, I'll reveal a science that, when learned and practiced aggressively, will allow you to go on the offensive, controlling and creating the interview the way you want it while answering all of the hiring manager's questions, often before he or she asks them. Think this sounds unreasonable? The science in this book teaches you to speak directly to a specific set of unconscious "questions behind the questions" that every hiring manager needs to be addressed and answered correctly. One of the secrets I'll reveal in this book is that the hiring manager often doesn't even know that he or she needs these questions answered. But I do!

I've witnessed these questions being answered—or not—during tens of thousands of hours of debriefing with hiring managers, some of the top executives in the country. I've heard these hiring managers tell me what they *really* want out of candidates but will never verbalize to you, the interviewee. These managers confided in me because I was a top performer, had built a deep trust with them, and earned their respect, giving me an inside view of their minds and how they think.

A master's degree in industrial psychology and counseling is another reason I was able to pull out secrets that no one ever had before (and probably never will again). Because I've put my experiences and knowledge into this book, you can gain these tens of thousands of hours of access, my eight-step science, and not-so-commonsense tips that will enable you to thrive and become an A-plus player in the business and game of interviewing.

In my nineteen-year career, I've had the privilege to recruit and consult for top companies all over the world. I've worked with many of the most accomplished CEOs, hiring managers, vice presidents, executive vice presidents, and scientists on the planet—people who are in the game of driving their companies or teams to achieve maximum results. During this time, I've hired in every discipline, including sales, technology, engineering, accounting, insurance, healthcare, and life sciences, among others.

After receiving many best-recruiter awards and plaques, I realized that someone needed my help even more than the companies for whom I'd worked. It was the candidate.

One of the tragedies of our time—and I've witnessed this again and again—is that qualified people aren't getting the jobs they should because they don't know how to interview. These candidates end up on the defensive, with no proactive, set strategy to win. It makes me so sad to see people memorizing over fifteen hundred possible interview questions and their coined "proper" responses when the solution is so much simpler.

So I've made it a personal mission to use my expertise to make sure that if someone has the experience, the skills and the temperament for a job—if they're *supposed* to get it—they will never fail due to simple inexperience at interviewing. My life is focused on helping candidates crack the code that's at work during the interview process, a code which many (including the hiring managers who are run by it) don't even know exists.

I've distilled these concepts into an eight-step process that allows interview candidates to take charge of the interview, be proactive instead of reactive, and win interviews based on their merits. Chapters 1 and 2 cover some critical, foundational basics you'll need to have mastered before moving on. Chapters 3 through 8 cover the eight-step REAPRICH practices in detail. The remainder of the book is devoted to in-depth examinations of some of the other factors that affect business success and personal well-being in today's world.

These concepts can't be found in normal job guides or traditional career sources. They stem from hard-earned experience and countless hours of interviewing. This system is an organized, effective way to make sure you accomplish everything you set out to do when you interview for that new job. If you spend time studying them, not only will you be prepared to represent your own skills and experience in the best possible light during an interview, but to stand out amongst your competition. Outside of marriage, life partnerships, and your choice of where to live, the decisions you make about your career are the most critical. Your job is your foundation—the driving force for your life. Even if you choose to work for yourself or start a business, representing yourself or your company in a way that differentiates you from everyone else out there is critical.

If you've spent years on an education or on learning your trade, even if you're an established executive, it's worth spending these few hours making a deep investment in yourself and your mastery of interview skills. Remember, I'm going to teach you top-level power skills that will dramatically differentiate you from every other candidate. I'm going to bring out your best so that you can put that front and center. I'm not here to just make you better, I'm here to make you phenomenal. Ongoing practice of the skills you learn here may help you outperform even those who are more educated or intelligent than you. In my experience, success is often more a matter of grit and hard work than skill.

I hope you'll take the challenge of finishing this book, applying the things you've learned daily, and making yourself into an expert interview candidate, the first, *crucial* step to a fulfilling career.

Warm regards,

Evan G. Pellett

CHAPTER 1

THE NECESSARY BASICS

"The real voyage of discovery consists not in seeking new landscapes but in having new eyes."
—Marcel Proust

If you're reading this book, you've taken a major step to becoming one of the elite few who'll have a unique level of understanding about the interview process. Through my experience as a top-level recruiter, I can offer an insider view that isn't available to guidance counselors or career coaches. There is no book on the market, no system other than this one, that actually offers insight into the minds of hiring managers from leading companies and gives you strategies to make those insights work for you.

INSIDER SECRET #1:

Self-sabotage is more destructive than any external factor. And it's more common than you might think.

Most career coaches have never spent time inside an actual corporation as a recruiter. As such, most of their information is outdated and learned from external sources rather than direct internal experience. The advice most colleges and career placement agencies offer is similar to what they offered fifteen years ago. In other words, it's not current, either. These colleges and career places mean well and do their best. Often, though, they can't give you more than the basics.

If you've been interviewing for some time without results, you may be battling feelings of discouragement. If you haven't yet dipped a toe in those waters but are contemplating a change of position or career, you may be anticipating the interview process with some degree of fear. Either one of these states can sabotage your success by undermining your confidence. If you follow the prescribed plan in this book, you'll begin to learn how to manage your emotional states and look within to conquer fear and doubt. You'll also discover that by practicing the methods in this book, you'll alleviate your fears and actually become energized and excited at the prospect of an interview, rather than fearful.

However, when you don't visualize success and practice enough to feel confident walking into the interview, you've sabotaged yourself before you've even begun.

DEFIANCE, THE SUBTLE SABOTAGE

You need to be willing to do a thorough job of interview preparation and show up as your best. If you're arrogant, defiant, or feel you can take shortcuts with the process in this book, then you fall into a group of people who often sabotage their own success. Subtle defiance is when part of you feels like doing less than necessary to succeed.

Some people employ subtle defiance because they don't like to be told what to do. Others do it because they're afraid of failure, so they create it in order to feel in control. Some people do it because they're afraid of their own success.

Usually, subtle defiance is unconscious. Showing up late, going out drinking the night before a big interview, not keeping agreements, and not practicing are ways to guarantee failure and help keep you in your safe zone. But your dream job and the interview process that gets you there are all about stepping outside that safe zone.

I once interviewed a recent Harvard graduate for a sales technology role. He was late for three interviews and wore knit booties and sloppy clothes to all of them. Each time he showed up he was more unshaven and his hair was greasier than the time before. He actually smelled of body odor. Amazingly, he'd actually won some technology contests at school, which is perhaps where he got his overblown sense of self-importance. The hiring manager commented to me that he had never interviewed someone who was so ill-prepared. I had the feeling that this young man arrogantly thought he was going to be the next Bill Gates. More power to him. He may have been hired elsewhere, but his attitude cost him a six-figure job at our firm.

CRACKING THE CODE: GETTING INSIDE THE MIND OF THE INTERVIEWER

Hiring managers have unconscious questions they need to have answered by each candidate. These unconscious questions fall into different categories: results and achievement; process, creativity, or working style; relationships; aggressiveness and energy; and like-ability. Here's the interesting part: most managers aren't even aware they're doing this! They've prepared questions to ask you during the interview, but often the things they *really* want to know are a secret even from themselves.

Unfortunately, most managers also receive very little interview training. Often they've been given the wrong diagnostic tools or questions to really determine if a candidate is a good fit for the job opening. Sometimes they've been given no tools whatsoever.

Here are a few of the types you're likely to meet in the course of your job search:

The Power Tripper: Disorganized and Uninformed

These managers are extra hard on candidates to prove their own intellectual prowess. They want to demonstrate their brilliance by stumping the person they're interviewing. Some make it an intellectual game to beat down candidates, or make them completely uncomfortable to see how they react. In sales, it is important to know how a candidate will react under pressure from customers. Unfortunately, unfair management interview practices sometimes take this tactic too far or apply it to positions for which it has little relevance. If you stay on the path I'm going to lay out for you, you'll be able to keep calm and stay focused even in the face of such an onslaught.

The Defensive Croucher: Motivated by Fear

Mediocre managers can be threatened by people they fear could do their jobs better. By applying the methods in this book, you actually control how managers see and feel about you, to dissolve their fears and reduce the chance they'll see you as a threat. They'll feel confident in you when you follow the proper steps in sequence and keep returning to those steps after answering each of their questions.

The Method Man: Relying on the Latest Interviewing Trend

In an effort to organize the interview process and identify strong candidates, some companies have adopted practices that involve looking for candidates to respond in a specific manner to specific questions. One popular example is known by the acronym STAR: Situation, Task, Action, and Result. For example, "I needed information for a trade show (Situation), so I had to do this (Task). The Action I took was this, and here was the Result." Managers who use this type of script and others like it feel that they're getting concrete examples rather than mile-high answers. Once again, if you're following the methods in this book, you should be able to answer a lot of those questions before they arise.

The Rogue Agent: Following a Secret Agenda

Many managers who haven't had specific interview training also do what I call "rogue" interviewing. This is where they base the interview on untested logic or idiosyncratic factors. These managers are the most dangerous kind because they bring judgments into interviews that are unfounded, unrelated, or copied from someone they deem knowledgeable. Some managers will look down on people who attended a certain school or certain type of school, grew up in a certain town, even practice a certain hobby, like golf or violin. They may have had one bad experience with someone from a certain background then generalized that experience to all people with that background. They also may have heard a generalization such as "Golfers aren't tenacious; they're more relaxed," or, "Runners aren't playing a team-oriented sport, so they're lone wolves." I've seen senior vice presidents ask a candidate if he was a "beer and Porsche guy or a Bentley and Champagne guy." I knew a CEO who believed you weren't working hard enough if you had time to play golf. Never mind that leisure activities are necessary for a healthy, balanced life, his attitude ignores the fact that many deals are cut on the golf course. With these managers especially, if you are not directing the interview, they'll grasp on to anything to make a judgment. They're often doing the best they can and may be great people; however, they want to feel safe that they've made a knowledgeable decision and will often attach to unproven logic to accomplish that.

If you allow this type of manager to direct the interview, you open the door for the hiring manager to fall back on faulty logic in determining your worthiness. You can't control someone else's unconscious prejudices, but you can be so persuasive, impressive, and confident that those illogical biases are swept aside.

Because of this and many other factors, candidates need a plan that works in rough going. This plan must differentiate you, build rapport, connect with a manager's unconscious mind-set, and address problem areas before that manager goes on the offensive with questions designed to disqualify you.

What if you could answer all of the hiring manager's unspoken, unconscious questions without them knowing you were doing it? You'd be doing them a huge favor. If you could cover all their critical areas through statements you offered unprompted and respond to the occasional questions with appropriate answers, you'd have 90 percent of the interview won.

How do you do that? With an eight-step plan that goes by the acronym REAPRICH.

REAPRICH =
RESULTS
ENERGY
ATTITUDE
PROCESS
RELATIONSHIPS
INTERVIEW THE INTERVIEWER
CLOSE THE INTERVIEWER
HUMANITY

This is more than a road map; it's a science. No matter where you are in your career, this science applies to you. The proactive strategy of REAPRICH has become the foundation for the most successful candidates interviewing today (some of whom will be competing with you for the same positions). It's a formula for becoming an enlightened, advanced, strategic, and proactive candidate. Employing REAPRICH will enable you to acquire the monetary gains, intrinsic rewards, personal growth, and ultimate satisfaction that comes from having your best career. This book is designed to help you get yourself that career.

TESTING AND VALIDATION OF REAPRICH

If scientific proof is achieved when results are both measurable and repeatable, then REAPRICH qualifies as the proven science of interviewing. I've tested it on C-Level executives (the highest-ranking corporate chiefs) as well as salespeople, engineers, sports medicine therapists, medical professionals, life science researchers, financial services workers, and many others. This includes vice presidents and senior vice presidents from all major industries and people of all ages, demographics, and cultures, whether they're skilled experts or interviewing for their first jobs right out of school. They've graduated from Harvard, MIT, the University of Massachusetts, Johns Hopkins, Salem State College, and many prestigious universities and vocational schools across the country.

These diverse professionals all have one thing in common: they worked to assimilate the lessons in this book, applied them to their own experience, and used them to win career-defining interviews.

Earlier, I said that REAPRICH would get you 90 percent of the way to the winner's circle. In the next chapter, we'll talk about that other 10 percent: avoiding commonsense mistakes that can sink even the most qualified candidate.

THE NECESSARY BASICS WORKSHEET

1. Use the space below to write down three times in which you self-sabotaged your own efforts. Sometimes the mere act of identifying your own past habits can help you identify and prevent them in the future.

CHAPTER 2
CRITICAL COMMONSENSE INTERVIEW PREPARATION

"Not to go back is somewhat to advance,
and men must walk, at least, before they dance."
—ALEXANDER POPE

Before we get into the specifics of the eight-part REAPRICH plan that you'll use to guide your actions to ultimate success in your interview, it's important to review a few fundamentals. These are principles that apply to every job applicant, in every industry, at every level. It's all about preparation and presentation.

BEFORE THE INTERVIEW

Know the names and backgrounds of the people who will be interviewing you. Many executives from top consulting companies like to begin an interview with the question, "So what do you know about me?" If that's the case, you'd better have an answer. They want to know you'll prepare for meetings with billion-dollar clients if they hire you. Information about personnel can often be found on the LinkedIn website or by calling the person who scheduled your interview, who may be able to supply a bio or give you a brief summary.

The interviewer may also ask, "Why do you want to come to work for this company?" Again, you need an answer that's based on specifics; show that you've done your homework. **So research the company's products and results**, both current and past, along with its product segments and services.

Know who the company's competitors are. It's all a part of coming prepared to show that you know the business and the market environment in which it operates.

Just as you would research the hiring manager or interviewer, **find out as much as possible about the backgrounds of the people you will be working for**, as well as the senior executives of the company. Once again, LinkedIn is a good place to start. Most companies list the bios of their vice presidents, senior vice presidents, and C-level executives on their websites.

People love to be recognized. **Find out if anyone you are meeting with has won awards, published articles, or done other things that have somehow distinguished them.** If you have friends or contacts at the company, ask them to fill in the blanks or gather some information on these people for you.

All of this preparation has a dual purpose. It will make you shine in the interview, but it will also tell managers that you've done your homework and have come prepared.

Polish up your résumé. Details on formatting this all-important tool appear in chapter 13.

Update your profiles on LinkedIn and any job search websites specific to your industry. If you don't have a LinkedIn account with a detailed profile, get one! LinkedIn is actually being substituted for résumés at many companies. You're not considered a player in the executive job search game if you're not current there—in fact, you may as well be invisible. As I write this, Indeed.com, Jobcase.com, and SimplyHired.com are good sites for those looking for blue-collar jobs and those that don't require a degree, but keep in mind that new sites are coming online all the time. Many recruiters do multiple searches on job sites daily to find top talent. Staying active on LinkedIn will also connect you with people in your field; you may even encounter the person who'll become your next boss.

Be tenacious. Once you've identified a position or company you want to work for, be persistent in pursuing an interview, then show up ready to perform. Don't stop trying after the first (or the second or the twentieth) "no." Stay in contact and keep reiterating your interest in the position, but do it in a respectful way.

I remember when I got into recruiting. I called the man who would eventually hire me almost every day for six months. I met with him several times during that period, and every time I was polished, wearing my nicest suit and tie. Although I was deeply inexperienced, he began to notice my polish and tenacity. After six months he called me and gave me a chance. Once there, I outworked all of the senior recruiters and within six months was his number one employee. When I would thank him for the opportunity, he'd always say to me, "It's not that I gave you the opportunity, it's what you did with it."

THE DAY OF THE INTERVIEW

Dress neatly and professionally. This means shining your shoes every time. I know a senior vice president in New York who wouldn't hire or do business with anyone who hadn't shined their shoes. He said, "If they show up to see me looking that way, that's how they'll look when they visit our clients!" You might be wearing an expensive suit, impeccably tailored, but if your shoes are scuffed, you'll look like a slob. I worked with another man who was well-dressed but came to our first meeting with white paint on his watch. (He'd been painting over the weekend and hadn't thoroughly cleaned up afterwards). These grooming mistakes show a lack of preparation and attention to detail. If you want a job that's a "ten," show up looking the part! If you have fitness issues that are addressable, get busy. Not only do hiring managers make judgments about your fitness for the job based on your physical fitness, being in shape is just a good life practice. There's no excuse for not maximizing your potential on all levels.

You absolutely need to be on time, and for our purposes, that means early. There is no acceptable reason to arrive later than ten minutes *prior to* your scheduled start time. Not only does that give you extra coverage for any delays you could experience due to traffic or unforeseen events, but you'll also arrive looking—and feeling— calm, fresh, and in control. Arriving early will also give you ten or fifteen minutes to spend in the parking lot meditating on the positive outcome of your interview.

Furthermore, most hiring managers will severely penalize or even discharge you from the interview process for tardiness. I don't care if you're interviewing or already have the job: if you have an issue with tardiness, fix it fast. Senior executives frown on people who walk in after a meeting has started, causing a disruption. I discussed defiance in the last chapter. Defiance is often a predecessor to lateness. If you can't leave old habits behind, you may not be successful in any career that calls for professional excellence.

Offer a firm handshake when greeting people, and look them in the eye. A weak handshake instantly takes away your credibility. Show you are intense, ready, and here to succeed!

Have hard copies of your résumé for every person you meet during your interview. Carry them in a black binder, not in a purse or anyplace they would need to be folded. Make sure the résumé matches the version you initially sent to them.

While waiting for the interview, **smile at the administrative assistant or receptionist in the lobby, and make sure you are especially polite to him or her.** Make small talk if the situation arises, keeping to positive subjects. Many hiring managers ask the people at the front desk whether interviewees were pleasant upon arrival. Companies want to make sure you treat people with respect.

I once saw a top salesperson lose a chance at a great job because he was mean to an administrative assistant who was scheduling his travel. Word got to the senior vice president of sales who simply said, "We wouldn't want anyone acting that way to our customers. Don't hire him."

Check your appearance in the bathroom once you enter the lobby of the building. I've seen people spill coffee or breakfast on their clothes, or come into an interview not knowing their hair had picked up leaves on a windy day. I once had an applicant come in with food on his tie. The people interviewing you will shy away from pointing out things like that because they don't want to insult you. However, it will still affect their perception of you in a negative way.

Don't be overly flashy in your dress or appearance. Be neat and properly dressed—power-dressed, if you will. Also make sure your clothes are ironed. Don't imagine that dressing "creatively" is the way to stand out in an interview. Your differentiation will be in your results and interview skills, not in some funky outfit.

Employers are looking for polish and conformity with a sense of class. Always dress one level up from the environment the company requires for its employees. (If you've done your homework as suggested before, you should know what the dress codes and work environment dictate.) I believe both men and women should wear a business suit to every interview. You're there to show that you exemplify excellence in all you do, to go above and beyond, and to show commitment to the employer. Honor the fact that they brought you there today. That doesn't mean you should wear a suit on a golf outing if that's your first meeting. If the setting is more casual, choose a button-down shirt and pressed khakis or linen trousers for men; a skirt or dress (appropriate for day wear—not cocktail or club attire) or a blouse and tailored pants for women.

> **INSIDER SECRET #2:** Hiring managers will judge you on a whole host of factors that have nothing to do with job performance or experience. Proper preparation will help you avoid missteps that can sabotage your chances.

Your accessories should match the way you're dressed. Don't bring your dad's briefcase from his first job in 1965, no matter how proud you are of the fact that he ended up CEO of the company. Don't bring grandmother's pocketbook either. You may be able to deviate from best practices once you have become an expert in your field but not when you're selling yourself at the outset.

Do not discuss personal problems, family, or bad experiences with past employers. Don't discuss your personal life at all, except if asked. (More on the proper way to talk about outside interests and hobbies in chapter 8.)

Smile, show warmth and kindness, and behave respectfully even if you have a sharp-edged business personality. The arrogant person rarely gets the job by acting that way during an interview.

Ask for business cards from the people you encounter throughout the interview process, from the receptionist who greets you at the front desk to the hiring manager who performs the interview, so that you can send follow-up notes to each person in the mail afterward.

AFTER THE INTERVIEW

Send thank-you notes. Send them to everyone who was involved in getting you the interview at the company, including any inside contacts or friends who helped set it up, the receptionist or scheduler who set your meeting, and of course everyone who participated in the interview itself. See chapter 8 for more detailed information on writing thank-you notes.

If you and the manager didn't discuss next steps, and you haven't heard anything in the two business days following your interview, place a follow-up phone call. This should be to the hiring manager who interviewed you only. If you can't get him or her on the phone, leave a voice message expressing your interest in one sentence, and ask about next steps.

Now that we've built a foundation, we'll move on to the eight-step REAPRICH process, the way to turn yourself into a powerful and successful candidate.

INTERVIEW PREPARATION WORKSHEET

Find a job listing you might be interested in and do some research as though you are preparing for an interview. Jot down some responses to the following questions:

1. Who will be interviewing you, and what can you find out about this person/these people?

2. Who are this company's competitors?

3. Who will you be working for and with, and what can you find out about them?

4. What can you add to your résumé and LinkedIn profile to bring it up to date?

5. What will you wear to the interview?

CHAPTER 3

RESULTS, ENTHUSIASM, AND A POSITIVE ATTITUDE: YOUR FIRST THREE KEYS TO CRACKING THE CODE

*"In the depth of winter, I finally learned that within
me there lay an invincible summer."*
—Albert Camus

Now that we've covered basic, commonsense interview preparation, the fun really begins. This is where we begin our exploration of the REAPRICH science that will allow you to go on the offensive and create the outcome of your interviews. With this science and a precise plan, you'll begin to lose your fear, have confidence, and never get lost while interviewing.

We'll start with "R" for Results, "E" for Energy and Enthusiasm, and "A" for Attitude, presented together because the force of these elements working in concert are very powerful.

When you go into an interview, the manager who spends time with you wants to know first and foremost: What is it that differentiates this person from everybody else I'm going to speak to today? This manager has already seen so many résumés for this opening. Some opportunities I've recruited for have generated as many as ten thousand résumés over the course of the search. Just as your results are going to appear at the top of your résumé (more on that later), they're also going to appear at the very beginning of your interview.

Results are what differentiate you from everyone else. You need to come up with a collection of six to ten achievements you've had that you can list in ninety seconds or less, depending on experience. Not stories, just statements of fact that are moving, defining, and exciting.

Here's where "E"—Energy and Enthusiasm—comes in. You need to have passion and enthusiasm as you deliver your results to a manager. Energy is the most important foundation for effectively communicating your results.

INSIDER SECRET #3:

Hiring managers will fail you during an interview for a lack of energy and enthusiasm. They will also fail you if they can't determine quickly that you have produced strong results in the past. If either of these factors are not evident and solid, they'll lose interest quickly.

Think about the last time someone got you excited about something. Now imagine the most energetic and enthusiastic person you know. You'll need to bring that kind of energy and excitement to every interaction in your interview process. People sometimes get jobs based on energy and charisma alone, because everyone loves someone who gets them excited or changes how they feel.

The energy and excitement you bring to the start of the interview sets the tone for the rest of your meeting. How will you get across those key things you need to communicate to make yourself a top-tier candidate? If you're unable to get that hiring manager's attention right away, you run the risk of his or her attention starting to wander. You want the interviewer to be present and attentive to you from start to finish.

While you want to show passion and energy, make sure you do it in a way that aligns with that company's culture. Keep in mind that if you're looking for opportunities in the engineering field, for example, or if you're pursuing an opportunity with a company that's perhaps on the conservative side, the hiring managers may be used to dealing with people who have a more understated demeanor. You can't jump up on a table at a conservative company and yell, "I'm so glad I'm here! You guys are great!" That's really not going to fly. But if you can bring some excitement to people who are in jobs they're not enjoying—if you can bring some juice and some freshness to what they're doing, some sunlight—you're going to make a lasting impression.

Hand in hand with energy is the "A" in REAPRICH: Attitude. Whereas Energy/Enthusiasm speaks to your outward presentation, Attitude speaks to your inner landscape. In order to be successful, you must find the intrinsic motivation that can only come from a positive attitude. In life there will always be setbacks; there will be missteps. If you can show that you can work through your problems and see your failures as learning opportunities, you will be able to sustain your enthusiasm to stay on track for as long as it takes to succeed.

Your attitude matters not just because it will color everything you do and say during your interview, but because managers are now actively looking for a positive attitude as part of the interview process. They want you to demonstrate grit, tenacity, and focus in your work results and also in your delivery. Large, well-respected companies have fired high performers for not being respectful of underlings or coworkers. Jack Welch, chairman and CEO of General Electric, implemented a "no jerk" policy at that company, and many others are now following suit. This means that no matter how intense, awkward, or direct you are or need to be, you can deliver any communication with kindness and respect. Overt ways of communicating must be warm and nonconfrontational, without undertones of covert passive aggression.

One of the things I've found helpful in keeping my own attitude in check is taking ownership. By that I mean holding myself accountable for both my successes and my failures. This is empowering because it puts us in the driver's seat. Whatever comes, we know we can not only handle it but ultimately use it to our advantage. Believing we can get better with time, even improve our IQ over time, is a *growth* mindset. By contrast, blaming our failures on other people or circumstances, believing ourselves to be at the mercy of bad luck, bad timing, or fate, is a *victim* mindset that can only hinder our chances for success. It's important to always look for the version of events wherein we are *accountable*, acknowledging our personal responsibility in the outcomes we create.

The power of results, delivered with energy and a positive attitude, is that managers feel more positive toward candidates when they're convinced that the person has achieved or, even better, overachieved. That gives the managers a comfort level—a sense of peace that they've made a good hiring decision. How they go about discerning whether or not you're that person is a mental process even the managers themselves may not understand.

THE SECRET: THE QUESTIONS BEHIND THE QUESTIONS

Managers will usually ask you a prepared set of questions in an interview, but for each manager there is also a set of questions *behind* the questions that are absolutely critical to the process. This is what is referred to as mental schema. One critical question is, "As a manager, can I feel secure that this hire will not fail me? Even better, can I be sure that the hire will substantially overachieve for me?" A clear, concise, and energetic recitation of your results will satisfy these concerns.

So how do you go about preparing a list of results that will be compelling and powerful?

You need to find a way to measure your work experience even if you're not currently in a job where your performance is measured in a specific way, even if you don't get performance reviews or career coaching. For example, what awards have you won? What percentage of results have you achieved? What things have you done—accomplishments, articles, discoveries—that have distinguished you in your field or the field you're trying to get into? Did you bring a project in ahead of budget? Did you save the company money? Did you organize something or pull off an event? These are all the types of things that should be a part of your results statement.

Not everyone has top-caliber results, so you may need to look in your background to identify the winning things that differentiate you.

Here are some questions that will help you come up with a results list:

- Have you ever been named Employee of the Month?
- Have you written an article? (It doesn't need to be a national publication; a company or industry newsletter counts!)
- Did you finish a project ahead of time? How many projects?
- Did you finish any projects under budget?
- Did you get rated an A or top 1 percent in your group, top 5 percent, or top 15 out of two hundred in the country?
- Did you develop a specialized program, cure, or accounting system?
- Have you done something no one else at your company has?
- Did you overachieve in athletics, a club, or in volunteer work?
- Did you get asked to be the lead for a special implementation?
- Did you make a discovery that saved money?
- Did you bring in or save a relationship that made the company money?

If there are no examples of excellence in what you've done during the last five years, then you need to ask, "Why not? Why haven't I won an award or overachieved? What do I need to shift or change in myself so that I do?"

Once you have your list of results, be sure it's featured prominently on your résumé, too. While managers do look at résumés, more often than not they just take a quick glance. So the first two bullets of your experience under each section of your résumé need to highlight your results. Where did you differentiate yourself? What makes you special? Why should a manager talk to you instead of everybody else asking for this opportunity? I've often interviewed people who have been number one or number two at their job in the world or who have won awards at the company they've been with, but those results are not anywhere on their résumés, nor do they come up when I speak with them on the phone or in person.

PRESENTING YOUR RESULTS IN THE INTERVIEW SETTING

When you walk into an interview, you'll normally find two types of managers. The first type jumps right into the interview, while the second type spends some time—maybe five minutes—building rapport. That manager may take this time because you know someone in common, or have a friend that referred you. They may also be testing your ability to loosen up and build rapport quickly. So if a manager chooses to build rapport, you want to be able to spend that time talking easily. Keep the initial introductory five-minute conversation high-level and brief to create a connection. If you go on talking too long, the manager will notice that. Keep your answers short, interesting, and fact-based, with no long stories out of the gate.

If a manager chooses to jump right into the interview, you want to be able to get right into that process as well, by presenting your results list you've prepared and practiced. It's key that after whatever small talk begins the interview, you jump deeply and quickly into your results statement right after. Don't wait to be invited: that invitation will likely never come. Remember, your results statement is answering the question behind the question, the one the hiring manager might not even know she has. So take the initiative.

Many people come into an interview and sit quietly or meekly in their chairs. It's critical to display energy, enthusiasm, and excitement. You need to light up the room when you walk in the door. Whether you're talking to a senior manager, a vice president, or a CEO, you've got to be present and engaged. They have to *feel* your energy. If you talk about results without energy, it's like collecting wood for a campfire and not bringing matches. Instead, you'll reach a point in the interview where you're rubbing two sticks together, trying to create a spark.

Do not pretend to be an expert on something you're not in order to impress a manager or build rapport. I once had an applicant say he was an expert French speaker. The manager said later, "He claimed to be an expert in French but he's kind of an intermediate. I think he's full of it; we probably shouldn't hire him."

PRACTICE MAKES DYNAMIC

There are very few people for whom all this energy, enthusiasm, and self-promotion comes naturally, particularly in an interview setting where they're nervous and invested in the outcome. But you have to break through your comfort zone to create an effective and powerful delivery. I often spend time watching people in mock interviews and giving them feedback until they perfect their interview presence, including persona, tone, and body language.

Practice smiling and showing excitement in the mirror before going in to meet with people. It's okay to feel awkward or nervous the first several times you do this—in fact, it's helpful. Much better to dispense with the butterflies in the privacy of your own home than in an actual interview! Practicing your interview delivery at least five times with a friend or family member can also be very valuable. Make sure you pick someone who is truly on your side and will neither spend all their time either criticizing or praising. The best choice would be someone you might initially feel a little uncomfortable around so that you can have the experience of starting over as needed, gaining confidence along the way. It's much better to get the jitters out and perfect a smooth delivery in a safe, controlled environment than it is in the actual interview process.

Think of it like a performance. If you had to sing a song in front of an audience, wouldn't you practice it multiple times?

Once you've got it down, your results statement amounts to a power pitch that you can deliver spontaneously and with passion not just in an interview but anywhere, at any time. Remember, you never know when you're going to meet someone who's a lead to your next job, or even your future boss.

EXAMPLES OF RESULTS STATEMENTS

Your results statement will be unique to you—it's what sets you apart. For clarification, here's an example of what it might sound like: "I've been a top 1 percent performer over the last three years, finished two major projects 20 percent ahead of time and 10 percent under budget. I was selected to evaluate all the financial software vendors, and I saved the company over fifty thousand dollars in one quarter by finding a mistake that had been overlooked in tracking. I also streamlined our shipping procedure."

Read that aloud. You'll see that it takes about twenty seconds to communicate something that will make a manager say, "Wow! This person is impressive." Someone else may have more experience or a better education, but if you can communicate how you differentiated yourself and added value to your company, an employer is much more likely to hire you.

A salesperson coming in for an interview might say something like the following: "Great to be here today. Thank you for your time. I was the number one salesperson for the East Coast division for e-commerce for the last three years. I won the President's Award in 2014. I've led two successful teams in the last year and a half, winning the team award from the Executive Club. I've also been able to break into one hundred and sixty-five new accounts over the last four and a half years, putting our company in first place out of all the other ERP competitors. Throughout the last ten years, I've been in the top 5 percent of achievement, and I won two President's Awards in 2005 and 2010."

Here's an example from my own career: "I've consistently been a top 1 percent achiever. I won the Oracle Best Recruiter award and three outstanding achievement awards. I also was ranked number one worldwide recruiter for both Oracle and Siebel Systems, and duplicated those results in many other companies. I've built top employee referral programs and increased employee referrals by over 500 percent in some cases, while also doubling new revenues as a COO within my first twelve months after the company had experienced four years of flat growth. I built specialized teams for Larry Ellison, the CEO of Oracle, that focused on selling into the top four hundred Golden accounts."

Congratulations! You've got their attention. Now you're going to move immediately to the next part of the REAPRICH formula: Process.

RESULTS, ENERGY, AND ATTITUDE WORKSHEET

1. Practice your results presentation in the mirror five times a day for five days. Concentrate on delivering it with energy and enthusiasm.

2. Once you feel secure about your performance in the mirror, practice your results five times in front of other people.

3. Write down any instances where you've gotten into trouble because of your attitude, or someone described your communication as brash, not warm, or unwelcome. Read these aloud to yourself, then write down ways you could have handled each situation better. If you feel you're unable to overcome ingrained, negative ways of being, you may need to seek outside help, for instance from a counselor, religious leader, or trusted mentor.

CHAPTER 4

PROCESS: A SPOTLIGHT ON CREATIVITY AND SOLID PRACTICES

"We know what a person thinks not when he tells us what he thinks, but by his actions."
—ISAAC BASHEVIS SINGER

Once you've begun the interview with a results statement of no more than ninety seconds, go right into the "P" step of REAPRICH: Process. Process simply explains how you achieved your results.

Understanding a person's pathway to excellence is a greater chance to create a long-lasting connection and deep relationship with them.

Many managers will think, "Oh, that's great. He's gotten results. I'm really excited. But how did he get there? Did he beg, cheat, borrow, and steal? Or can he talk to me about integrity and great processes for getting to those results?"

Your process statement should follow your results with no more than a two-second pause. Succinctly articulate

> **INSIDER SECRET #4:**
> Fear of the unknown is a huge unconscious motivator. If a hiring manager doesn't understand *how* you got to your results, she may not trust the positive impressions she's formed so far.

and discuss the processes you used, developed, or put in place that allowed you to get phenomenal results. If you've done great things, managers want to understand how you got there.

A good manager will think about how your process may work within the context of his own job:

- Am I familiar with some of these methods?
- Could I add these methods to my team?
- Have I wanted to add these methods for a while?
- Can there be a "wow factor" associated with this process that will make me look better to my higher-ups?
- Can this candidate teach me how to get these phenomenal results?

You're in great shape if the manager ends up saying, "I want you on board so you can do this for me or my team. I want this to be a part of our skill set and our arsenal as we move forward as an organization."

Let's use my career as a recruiter as an example this time. I'd begin with, "Listen, it's great to be here today, and I appreciate your time. I was a number one worldwide recruiter for four Tier One companies …" I'd finish my results statement, then go right into: "The way I did this was cold calling more than anyone else on the team. I was also there earlier each day. I set up programs for employee referrals that people would get excited about. Sometimes we gave away an automobile. We gave away things that people wouldn't buy for themselves. We did that because we found that if we gave them money, it didn't generate the same excitement as offering them a new experience. These programs cut recruiting budgets by 50 to 75 percent.

"We also created sourcing programs where we researched and acquired names and phone numbers of the best people in the world. We found out how to get them excited—without being threatening or direct, of course. I also developed and taught ways to sell the company's vision and how to brand that company. And if they didn't have a strong brand or something that was a 'wow factor' about the company, we put together all the key pieces and made sure we spoke about that and got it right into people's minds the minute we got on the phone with them. I created a program focused on security, opportunity, and possibility in ways that locked in top candidates. We said, 'Let me tell you about Oracle. It's the number one company in the database world. They have more opportunities than anywhere else to learn each type of technology that is cutting edge, strategic.' This set us up to have instant credibility.

"I found out, too, the most effective way to utilize job boards, how to write really powerful marketing messages and ads so that people wanted to come to the company. So that's a little bit about my process."

The process portion of the interview is the best place for demonstrating your creativity. I don't mean creativity as in artistic ability. I'm talking about creating something unique that helped you get to your results or showed a high level of thinking. An example: A manager from a top engineering company hired a man, in part, because he'd built a car during the summer between high school and college. He hired this bachelor's degree recipient over other candidates with PhDs because this candidate had demonstrated the ability to think and create. Creativity and its companion, curiosity, are top attributes that managers search for in candidates because it means they have the ability to learn, think, and explore.

Every manager looking to hire someone wants to gain a strong sense of how a potential employee does things, and how he or she reaches the achievements that we think of as outstanding or elite in the world. Effectively communicating that will put you head and shoulders above the crowd.

Next, we'll examine one of the most important aspects of business success and how it can help you ace the interview process: Relationships.

PROCESS WORKSHEET:

1. Write down a list of processes that support your results. Read them aloud to yourself in the mirror five times a day for five days.

CHAPTER 5

RELATIONSHIP BUILDING AND MAINTENANCE: PAST AND PRESENT

"A man is known by the company he keeps. A company is known by the men it keeps."
—Thomas J. Watson

After you've spoken about your results and your process, look at your interviewer, and pause for a moment to see if the manager has any questions. At this point, by merging your results and processes, you've accomplished about 55 percent of what you need to do: the critical goals of getting the manager's attention and communicating the key things you need to get across.

Remember, everyone who interviews you is sitting there thinking, "I've got this list of five or ten questions I need to get answered today." He may be anxious to get to those and wondering how you're going to handle the answers. If you've done your job well so far, he will be rooting for you, hoping you'll confirm the positive opinions he's already formed.

But a manager can spend all his time asking questions and dodging around the really important issues, which often happens when people don't stay focused. Once again, you're going to put things in order for him, actually doing the manager a favor. You're answering the questions behind the questions, the critical things managers need to know, before he even gets a chance to ask them.

So, after you've answered each question as concisely and thoroughly as possible, move immediately to your next place in the REAPRICH process. After Results, Energy, Attitude, and Process comes "R" for Relationships.

Anyone who is hiring wants to know three things about your relationships. First, that you're able to build them. In other words, can you play nicely with other people in the company? Managers want to know whether you can build the type of rock-solid, effective relationships that will allow you to maneuver within the organization, to create rapport with the customers the company is trying to do business with, and that allow people to see you as approachable. Second, they want to know whether you can sustain those relationships or whether you're someone who burns bridges, or turns against people after working with them for a time. The fact is, some people perform well in this area for short periods, but have a tendency to fall out with coworkers over time, either because of ego problems, poor work habits, lack of a cooperative spirit, or just a general inability to get along. That's a concern for managers because it can seriously disrupt an organization. Third, managers want to know that you will bring new and beneficial relationships to their company, whether it be customers, suppliers, vendors, or others.

INSIDER SECRET #5:
One of the biggest fears of hiring managers is having a personality conflict on their team. Showing that you have the ability to create and maintain relationships alleviates this fear.

Managers want and need to know that you can demonstrate a long-term track record of relationships that will benefit the business. Knowing this is another level of reassurance and answers another question behind their questions.

As an example, after discussing results and processes, you might say the following: "In terms of relationships, I have solid, long-standing contacts at ten of the major partners critical to your ERP business." Or, "I have relationships with four of the major companies that supply your manufacturing business." Or, "I have relationships with three of the scientists that can help us really look at this research and validate it as we take the company to the next level with this new product." Or, "I could bring a few people with me, or use them as resources."

MINING YOUR RELATIONSHIP NETWORK

Before you go in for your interview, think about anyone you know who might have a connection to this job. Take the time to write down a minimum of five—and as many as nine—relationships that relate to what the company you're interviewing with is doing. Be sure to include both short-term and long-term relationships in the list. A short-term relationship might be someone with whom you work now or someone you worked with at your last job. A long-term relationship might be anyone from a teacher or mentor who inspired you early in your career to a college roommate who's achieved success in business and is still in your life. Lately, I've noticed that some top companies are beginning to understand the value of building a corporate culture and are interviewing for qualities like "valuing others." This can be evident in your volunteer experience, so consider that area of your life when mining for connections.

Dig deep, and think about ways these relationships might be of benefit to a potential employer. Also think about ways your relationship with these people has helped your own professional development in demonstrable ways.

Here's an example from an experience I had counseling a writer who wanted to make a career move into editing. She was unsure about which relationships mattered, and how to talk about them in an interview. Her case is instructive, because it demonstrates a way of thinking about relationships, and shows how to distill a relationship story into a manageable interview "sound bite." Here's the story she told me about her first editor:

"My mentor is the editor-in-chief of a well-regarded trade magazine, and had been for about twenty years when we first met. She's very successful and very well liked; everyone in that industry knows her. Fifteen years ago we met at a writer's retreat where I now teach, but at the time we were both there as students, workshopping our novels. We both admired each other's writing, and we became friends. We saw each other every year at that same retreat, and kept in touch throughout the year between, sharing our works of fiction with each other. At that time, my 'day job' was writing advertising and PR materials. I'd often talk to her about my work, and I think she could see that I had a strong work ethic, was very responsible, and could work independently. A few years later, when she left the position she'd been in to start a new magazine, she hired me. She was taking a chance because she knew I had never done that specific type of writing before. But I think she had confidence in me both because she liked my fiction writing and because of what she had learned about my character and my seriousness toward my work."

That's a great relationship story. It shows how the connection was created, how it shifted from the personal to the professional, and showcases some of the writer's best attributes. But it's too long and unfocused for an interview setting. I suggested that the writer focus on her results and processes to distill it down to its essence. Here is the final relationship script she came up with: "I met my mentor at an Oregon Writers Colony retreat, where she saw my skill set and witnessed my work ethic firsthand. She saw something special or original in my writing style. This resulted in her hiring me as an editor for *Wedding Photographer* magazine **even though I had no editorial experience.** Working with her has helped me develop strong editorial skills, and she's introduced me to so many influential people in the world of publishing. She continues to be a mentor and a great source of information and contacts that I'll be able to draw on in my work here at Pendant Publishing."

In addition to long-standing outside relationships, there may be someone within the company with whom you have a relationship, someone you know well. Use that. There's nothing more important or valuable than a strong internal reference. If the manager knows the person who referred you, discuss that. What would the person say about you? Get an informal reference from that person in advance that you can email to the manager, or give the person a call to talk about the business in preparation.

However, if you're going to give a manager an internal reference, you need to go one step deeper. You need to know that your reference is valued by that manager and the company. If not, you don't want to bring that person's name into your hiring process. Find out about your reference's status within the company by asking him or her some probing questions, such as, "How's the year been? How have you done? Any promotions on the horizon? What were your results last year?" You'll need to do some very in-depth research before you make that connection for yourself.

You also want to make sure that reference will say great things about you when asked. Don't assume that because someone is a friend, he or she will have your best interests at heart. I've seen people give references that ended up not giving them favorable reviews. Strange, yes, but it does happen, for a variety of reasons—including jealousy.

The whole interview process is about continually creating positive connections in the hiring manager's mind. Because if the manager feels good and excited about working with you, he or she is most likely going to make a decision in your favor. Throughout this process, it's important to respect and honor the personality types of the managers you encounter. For instance, analytical people who crunch numbers all day often seem to enjoy someone that moves them emotionally. This is because they spend most of their day thinking and problem-solving, often feverishly.

A very successful salesperson in my family once told me "I get to know everyone from the guys on the loading dock up to the CEO and treat them all the same way. Remember, every human being has dignity."

I also think about the relationships my dad built throughout his career. He began as a chemical engineer, worked his way up to technical sales specialist, and, eventually, regional manager, winning recognition for being the top salesman in the country many years in a row. He honored everyone from every background and economic standing, and really showed me what being a true gentleman was all about. He had a way of making every person he spoke to feel valued.

When I was a boy, he took me to one of the paper companies his firm did business with. He had the most respectful relationship with the old gentleman who ran the boiler. It was hard, manual labor and this gentleman was grimy as a result. He had some missing teeth in front too, but he had my dad's full respect. I remember Dad climbing inside these big boilers and getting his hands dirty right alongside the guy. Sometimes, he'd come home smelling like pulp. Why? Because he had the commitment to do whatever it took to build the relationship and to win the business.

Once you get to the relationship portion of your interview, you'll want to take a little more time to elaborate on how you were responsible for building and nurturing each relationship, and how it relates to the job for which you're applying. Do not go off on tangents, however.

After you've discussed your relationships, pause to see if the manager has questions. Give her time to probe if she needs to. If you have a relationship in common, she'll probably want to ask questions about that. Give her the chance to spend that time. Answer her questions in a focused and direct manner, accentuating the positives about your relationships. Never validate a negative about someone, even if the manager brings it up. If that happens, gracefully deflect the issue by moving on to your next relationship or the next phase of REAPRICH.

Always remember to smile! Keep smiling, warm them up, because in the next phase you're going to turn the tables ...

RELATIONSHIPS WORKSHEET:

1. Write down two long-term relationships such as bosses, coaches, mentors, or friends (one which affected your career). Answer the following questions in writing for each: How did you secure this relationship? Was it through performance? How did this person become interested in you? How did he or she see positive qualities in you? How did you build and nurture this connection?

2. Write down two strong, short-term relationships such as coworkers, friends, or contacts from volunteer activities. Ask yourself the same questions.

3. Distill your notes down into two to four sentences that you can recite quickly. They should be rich with facts and cover short- and long-term relationships. Practice reciting these statements to yourself in the mirror for five minutes a day for five days.

CHAPTER 6

INTERVIEWING THE INTERVIEWER

"When people talk, listen completely. Most people never listen."
—ERNEST HEMINGWAY

People love to talk about themselves and are moved when you care enough to listen intently. People also respect someone with the courage to ask questions, without arrogance, but with genuine curiosity. That's why this next phase is so crucial: you're going to interview the interviewer.

Prepare a minimum of two questions—preferably four or five—that you can ask the hiring manager.

Don't ask questions for which you should already know the answers. Base questions on things that are relevant to the team or position you're going for, and make sure the questions will elicit a positive response.

> **INSIDER SECRET #6:**
> A manager wants to see that you have the courage to politely turn the tables on him to probe and extract information.

This is your time to demonstrate a depth of expertise or knowledge that may go deeper in probing the manager's mind and help begin to create solutions for him. Good managers will admire a great thought process and problem-solving ability. You want him to see you as intelligent, especially if you're working within the engineering field, as a technical person, or have a PhD.

The following are some examples of questions for your interviewer:

- Tell me about some of your most successful people. What's made them great?
- How can I help your team? What is the best way my skills could add value?
- If you hired me today, what would you have me help you and your team with in the first three months?
- What are great things about this company that I would only hear from you and may not find in my own research?

Those are some great questions to ask a hiring manager, because if the answers relate to things you've done or are interested in, you can also show a desire to help spearhead a project as a way of preclosing the interviewer. Also notice that these are all positive questions that will make the manager excited, thinking about his own successes and those of his team or company.

This manager will remember the emotional state in which you leave him. Don't go down the negative news tunnel unless he brings it up first. You don't want to open the door by asking something like, "Tell me about people who failed and why?" You don't want failure, or people who have failed, to be any part of your interview process, or be associated with a manager's thinking about you. If the manager brings up a negative topic, respond as briefly and neutrally as possible and move on.

Take your time during this phase. Ask questions about aspects of the job you're truly interested in and get the answers. Don't interrupt; instead focus, listen, and maintain eye contact. Make the interviewer feel you're present and that you're a good listener.

The manager will respect the fact that you have some questions about the company, rather than just walking in and saying, "Hey this place is great, I'll take it!" It makes you look discerning, with good judgment. It also implies that you have options, something else which makes you a more desirable candidate.

I'm not suggesting you play "hard to get" at your interview, or come across as arrogant. That's a mistake I often see. Rather than coming across as competitive in a healthy way, arrogance communicates the attitude, "I'm the best thing in the world and they need me." Not a good approach. Some people who don't have any results try to play that card, and it usually doesn't work out well.

Asking intelligent questions implies that you know before you show up who the interview is with—another reason to do your homework. What has the interviewer done that's special? Has this person been a top performer? If you don't have the information, find it. Top companies want to see that you've put in the energy and the research, that you've made the phone calls and gone on the Internet. It's not always easy, but keep in mind, compared to the amount of time you spent in school and in your career thus far, another three hours to prepare for an interview is really nothing. Even if it takes ten hours, being ready is worth it. This next step in your career could be the most critical one that you'll take this decade.

You begin to preclose an interview when you turn around one of the answers to your interview questions to ask the manager how your skills can benefit some of the needs the company has now. When the interviewer makes a correlation between your skills and the needs of the company and begins to see it happening, then you've begun to preclose. Here's an example:

> **YOU:** I have shared some of my strong skills and we have agreed on their value. Where would you put me first in your organization if I was to start today?

> **INTERVIEWER:** I think your tech skills with the Cloud could really help with our upcoming implementations. I would put you with Margie and have you sit through our software and progress evaluation meetings with her.

Building your preclose around three or four solid facts about your results, process, and relationships is like putting anchors in the manager's nervous system around these important attributes. The perfect preclose focuses on your results, reminds the interviewer how you picked up those skills, and makes him or her think about your potential to teach those skills to a team. "Given that I helped achieve a 90 percent acceptance rate among the retail division for our new POP systems by revamping the training protocols, how do you see me contributing to the rollout of your new POP terminals in the fall?"

Like everything else, you want to practice your precloses and your interview questions with someone else many times over. Next chapter: closing time!

INTERVIEWING THE INTERVIEWER WORKSHEET:

1. Following the guidelines in this chapter, write a list of six targeted questions for each interview. You want to use two different ones for preclose with each different interviewer. If there are more than three interviews you may substitute and reask two of the questions.

2. Write three possible precloses for each interview.

CHAPTER 7

CLOSING THE INTERVIEWER: ASK FOR THE JOB

"You gain strength, courage, and confidence by every experience in which you really stop to look fear in the face...You must do the thing you think you cannot do."
—Eleanor Roosevelt

The last step of the interview process is closing. Closing is a familiar concept in sales, so it's appropriate to apply it in this situation, where you are essentially "selling" yourself to a potential employer.

Whether or not you're going for a sales position, managers want to see that you have the courage to ask for the job! They want to see that you can take risks, and asking about the next steps in the interview process is one way to demonstrate that. If it is a sales opportunity, they want to see you ask for the job outright. They want to know you're not afraid to ask a customer for an order.

The closing process can happen on five or six levels, so it's important to think of it as a process, not a moment. If you don't get a job offer with the first close, that doesn't mean you should stop trying. When you're closing someone, you just want that person to move you forward to the next step. For example, early in the process, a light, gentle close might be, "I really enjoyed our time today. Can you tell me about what happens next in our process?" Or, "Should I follow up tomorrow or the next day?" Or even, "Do you have someone else you want me to meet with?"

In each of those examples, you are simply trying to get the manager to take another step forward in the interview process. Give him something he can say "yes" to. You can always back out of the closing stage and return to interviewing the manager to see if you can get to an answer that will provide an opening to close.

Once you find that opening, the interview will feel as though it's run its natural course. That's the time for a stronger close. Here are some examples:

- Do you see yourself extending me an offer today before I leave?
- Are you recommending me for hire?
- Will you be moving me on to the next steps in the interview process?
- Is there anything that would keep you from extending me an offer today?
- Are you going to offer me the job today?
- Is there anything else I would need to do before you would offer me this opportunity?
- I've got some other opportunities I'm looking at, but I'm most excited about this company; I really hope to get an offer here.
- Do you see us moving forward to the offer stage where I can be a part of your team?

Or, "I really enjoyed my time today with you. Thank you for being so informative. I see a lot of benefits and value in your company. I'd really like to become part of your team. It's really a frontrunner in terms of the opportunities I'm considering. What do you see as a next step? Do you need anything from me, my references for instance? I can forward them to you later today so you'll have a chance to check them. I'm really trying to make a decision by Friday. Does that work for you?"

If the hiring manager seems noncommittal and doesn't want to give you an answer, start asking some probing questions. For instance, "Is there anything else I can tell you or expand on to help make you feel more comfortable with my experience?" Or, "Are there any areas in my background that concern you and might be reasons why you wouldn't hire me today?" Then pause and wait for an answer. Sometimes a manager wants to know about something but may not ask about it. That's why it's important to pause at the different stages. You want to answer the questions; you want to get the interviewer excited; you want to win the interview. However, you also want to give the manager time if he or she needs an answer to a specific question. Probe for concerns or objections, and if something comes up, address it before you walk out that door. You

INSIDER SECRET #7:
Many companies won't give you the job if you don't close the deal by asking for it. Hiring managers feel that if you don't have the courage to ask for the job, you won't have the courage to ask customers for their business. They also may feel that you won't be able to ask tough, direct questions when needed.

don't want to be thinking on the drive home, "Geez, I didn't feel like he was totally sold on me." It could have been something you said; it could also have been an area that you didn't cover.

You may have great skills in a specific area, but because that subject didn't come up in the interview, the hiring manager figures you don't have the experience. That's why you ask during close, "Are there any other areas that I can expand on in my experience?" Or, "Do you feel comfortable with how my experience fits with this job opportunity?" If the manager looks uncomfortable or doesn't say anything, ask the same questions again.

Closing is uncomfortable for most people, in part because they empathize overmuch with the interviewer; no one likes to be put on the spot. But think of it this way: managers who conduct job interviews deal with people all the time who aren't organized. That lack of focus can be very frustrating for a manager, who has a goal to achieve specific things within the time spent with you. So when you're organized, awake, and focused, and you get a manager to a point in the process where he or she feels good about the interview, you've made his or her day easier. You've done that person a favor. And you've done yourself a favor as well.

CLOSING WORKSHEET:

1. Write your closes, the ways you plan to ask for the job.

2. Practice your closes in the mirror. See and hear yourself asking the questions in an interview setting and visualize positive results.

CHAPTER 8
KEEPING IT REAL: THE IMPORTANCE OF HUMANITY

*"Too often we underestimate the power of a touch,
a smile, a kind word, a listening ear, an honest
compliment, or the smallest act of caring, all of which
have the potential to turn a life around."*
—LEO BUSCAGLIA

"H" for Humanity is the last step in the REAPRICH formula. The whole process, up to this point, has been about making connections. Humanity is about connecting on a more personal level. Think of it as the cherry on top of a layer cake of connection.

When following the first seven steps it's possible that you may finish your interview early. I often finish my own in thirty or thirty-five minutes, and the hiring manager, although he'd allotted an hour for the interview, finds he has no more questions for me. It's fun when he's not really sure what just happened but knows he is very excited about hiring you. You've done that manager a service. It's exhilarating for a manager to have all of his questions answered when he didn't even have to ask them—just as exhilarating as it is for you to have aced the interview.

However, this early finish can occasionally leave an awkward space in what had been scheduled as a longer interview. Fill that time by focusing on something human about the person. A picture on the wall is always a great topic for conversation. If you see he received an award for something or has boating or karate pictures, ask him about these interests. (Of course, you need to be sure that you're actually in the office of the person who's conducting the interview. This can be done by looking for something with his or her name on it.) If you can't find any personal clues about your interviewer, either online or in your surroundings, you can always say, "Tell me about you and some of your interests or hobbies." This is another way to create connection and get him to speak about himself. Getting to know him and creating a deeper connection can only help your chances. Don't get silly, lose focus, or be unprofessional. Don't spend this time talking mainly about yourself. Make it mostly about him. If he dismisses you from the interview early, that's fine too. In that case, don't try to stay and talk longer. The manager may be grateful for the extra time he now has to move on to other work.

He may also already be sold on you! Watch his cues. His facial expressions and body language will tell you if he feels the need to fill the hour talking with you, or is comfortable ending the meeting. Once the manager is sold on you, and is making a move to end the conversation, you should never keep asking for the sale. Offer your thanks, a hearty handshake, and make your exit. You're done! And well done, you.

Helping others is another aspect of humanity, and something we need more of in the world. So it's a good practice, once you have finished your interview, to go do something nice for someone else and take the focus off of yourself. This prevents you from indulging in fearful thoughts about the outcome of the interview. That tendency is natural—all the focus on self, self, self, which is so necessary while working the REAPRICH formula, has a darker flipside, one that can lead us to dwell on the negative, obsessing about the interview, and

INSIDER SECRET #8:
Interviewers are people too!

giving ourselves a case of the woulda-coulda-shouldas.

Instead, go help an old lady across the street or volunteer at a soup kitchen after your interview. Give away some time at the local Boys & Girls Club or usher a church service. Get out there and find a way to make a difference. Also begin to think of ways you can help your new boss and the company once hired.

We talked in chapter 2 about writing thank-you notes. Now is the time. Do this later the same day, and get them in the mail no later than two days after your interview, particularly if you did not get a clear statement from the hiring manager about next steps. Unless your handwriting is completely illegible, handwrite them; you want to show that you cared enough to make an effort. (One caveat: if you're a horrible—or even average—speller, compose the text on a computer and spell-check it, then hand-copy it once it's perfect.) Include one detail that's specific to what that person did for you ("Thank you for accommodating my schedule in setting up an appointment with Mr. Carson …") For those making the hiring decisions, include one reason why you're excited about working for the company. Try to make it a detail that came up in the course of your interview; that way the hiring manager knows he or she had your full attention and that you'll know how to follow-up on conversations with clients or suppliers.

All of these practices will help make you feel grateful. Gratitude is the attitude if you want to have great energy that will translate into every aspect of your life, both personal and professional.

HUMANITY WORKSHEET:

1. Write down three possible questions you can ask your interviewer based on your research about him or her.

2. Write down three things you plan to do after the interview to
take the focus off yourself and place it on making a difference
for others.

CHAPTER 9
RECAP OF REAPRICH STEPS IN ORDER

"Practice is the best of all instructors."
—Publilius Syrus

Don't quit now! Review and practice to be the best you can be. Effort, grit, and practice often outperform native intelligence. Practice also allows behaviors to become natural, requiring less thought. Once you've practiced REAPRICH, you won't have to stop to think about the parts of the process; it will become intrinsic to the way you conduct yourself.

Let's review up to this point …

R: Results, E: Energy/Enthusiasm, and A: Attitude
These first three elements are inextricably tied together. When you walk in the door for your interview, you should be ready to talk about your results. The manager is either going to spend a few moments building rapport with you, or will say something like, "Thanks for coming in today. Bring me up to speed on your experience." Your response: "Thank you for your time. I'm excited to be here!" Follow this with your practiced results statement. Make it quick—no more than ninety seconds—and concise.

As you talk, go back over the last ten years of your experience. For example, "I was number one at this company. I won an outstanding achievement award in 2012 at this organization. I built a top-performing team that won the company's President's Award five years prior to that, and I've been in the top 10 percent every year since, meaning I'm a very consistent achiever. I've been on the same accounts for the last fifteen years, so I have great rapport with my customers." Remember: your results should align with the first two bullets on your résumé.

You're going to deliver this information with energy and enthusiasm, which will be apparent from the moment you walk into the office wearing a warm smile and making eye contact with those who engage you. Because you've practiced, visualized success, and meditated on a positive outcome, your attitude is positive, and that shines through as well.

P: Process

Immediately go into explaining how you got to the results you just recited. What's your working style? What makes you better? Are you independent? Do you need a lot of handholding? (I would hope not, and that you don't say you do in the interview, though if you work better as a part of a team, that's something you could mention.) Are you collaborative when you need to be? Do you bring teams together to talk about things? Provide the manager with the information he or she needs to feel secure that you actually achieved those results, and that you have processes in place to replicate them in your new position.

At this point, you'll want to pause to give the interviewer a chance to ask questions about what you've presented so far. Answer any questions thoroughly but succinctly, then move directly on to the next step.

R: Relationships

What are the relationships you bring to the table? Who do you know that would be of value to the company? Can you bring other people with you to be part of the organization? Talk about the relationships you have, as well as your skills for building new ones, in a way the hiring manager will find exciting.

Let's say you've just graduated from college and have little or no work experience. That doesn't mean you have no relevant relationships. You might want to talk about some that you built playing sports, or perhaps via an internship you did to gain experience in a specific area.

INSIDER SECRET #9:
The most successful interview candidates aren't necessarily the most experienced, the most educated, or the most qualified for the job. They are the best prepared.

How did you differentiate yourself? Talk about what made you stand out in those opportunities, whether it was getting good grades in high school, participating in team sports, belonging to clubs, volunteering, or learning something about the company's field. Bring up things that will help the manager understand that you know how to build relationships and open doors.

Internal collaboration—getting people to do things for you in major companies and be part of your team so you can reach your goals—is a critical component of relationship building. You want the manager to think, "If I bring this candidate in, she's going to get along well with the team. This person's going to be able to forge relationships that involve bringing different parts of the organization together for approval."

Once you have covered Results, Energy/Enthusiasm, Attitude, Process, and Relationships, and the manager has a clear sense of these things, it's time to move to the point where you turn things around.

I: Interview the Interviewer

During this step, you'll utilize some of the thoughtful, intelligent questions you prepared beforehand, questions that will elicit positive responses from your interviewer.

Many managers are watching for this. They want you to do it; not in a cocky or arrogant way, but with genuine interest and curiosity. It tells the manager not just that you want to know more about the business, but that you took the initiative to find out enough about the company to ask cogent questions.

You can start by saying something like, "What made you decide to join this company? What are the key points from your personal experience here or that I might not see on the website?"

Project class and be polite, but be direct in the way you pose your questions. If you know that the company has had difficulty in a certain area, avoid asking about that, even though you may have opinions or ideas about what went wrong and how to fix it. If you have genuine concerns about that issue, this is not the place to bring them up. Research it on your own and decide whether or not it's a deal-breaker for you as a potential employee.

C: Close the Interviewer

After you finish interviewing the interviewer, you're going to close. This is where you begin to secure the job for yourself, where you get the manager to say yes, or where the company makes a commitment to you about becoming an employee.

If the manager is not willing to commit, seems to be on the fence, or won't give you an answer, it's important to know why. Return to interview mode and ask probing questions. "What kind of experience do you want to see beyond the job description?" is a good one. Or, "Is there some area of specialization you feel is important that we haven't talked about?" The manager may respond, for example, that the company needs someone with CAD experience. You may not have brought it up, but you have CAD experience. So you can say, "I started working with CAD in high school," and give quick, solid examples of where you have used it.

That's why probing is important. You would never have known that the manager had a concern about this area, but now you've covered the issue and laid any concerns or objections to rest.

Once you've done that, return to closing. Say, "That's great. I'm glad I could elaborate on that for you. Are there any other areas you'd like me to cover?" If the manager says, "No, actually, I feel good about you," that's an opening for a close. At this point, you might sum up things by saying something like, "I really like your background and how you run this team. I think I could learn a lot from you. I'm looking to grow as a person, to be mentored, and increase my knowledge base. Are you going to generate an offer for me to join the team?"

This is a way of asking direct questions and complimenting people at the same time. Be energetic and enthusiastic but don't fawn. As always, maintain a polite and professional demeanor.

H: Humanity

Humanity is the final step and may be as simple as giving someone a really warm handshake and smile and telling him how wonderful it was to meet with him. It could also be your beginning a discussion based on what you can derive personally about them from the walls of their office. Remember to take the focus off of yourself when leaving the interview and to visualize a positive outcome.

REAPRICH RECAP WORKSHEET

1. Write two positive outcomes you want to see in your life that the REAPRICH process can help you achieve: one personal and one professional.

CHAPTER 10
BUSINESS LEADER PRACTICES AND COMMONSENSE RECAP

*"Common sense in an uncommon degree
is what the world calls wisdom."*
—Samuel Taylor Coleridge

When all else fails, use common sense. Make sure your business practices are current, awakened, and productive. It's important to integrate this commonsense recap into your knowledge base the same way you've assimilated the REAPRICH process. Believe me, a misstep here can be a disaster.

First and foremost, always arrive at your interview location at least ten minutes early. After you arrive, find a restroom and check your appearance in the mirror. I can't tell you how many times I've seen people who've prepped at home, but arrive at the interview looking odd. They walk in and one side of their hair is sticking straight up. Or they've had something to eat beforehand and now they've got mustard on their cheek or a crumb in their eyebrow. I've seen people sit on something in their car—maybe a child left candy on the driver's seat—and then walk into an interview with chocolate melted to the side of their suit jacket. This type of mistake is completely avoidable. Look in the bathroom mirror, turn around, and make sure that your appearance is in order.

You want your appearance to be at its most polished. And speaking of polish, no matter who you are, what type of job you're applying for, or what type of company, your shoes should be polished and looking great when you're interviewing. In fact, even after you get the job you should always have your shoes polished. If someone is considering you for a promotion and looks down to see that your shoes are a mess, he or she is going to think, "Gee, I don't know. He didn't take the time to be thorough." People are looking for the little extras. They want you to look good whenever and wherever you're representing the company.

Outside of corporate America, there are many jobs and careers where polished shoes aren't as big a concern. But as someone who has risen through the ranks to become a top manager, I can assure you that many people have strong feelings about this. Grooming, polished shoes, all of these things are critically important. That first impression is a key one. Even if you're going in for your fifth interview, double-check these things.

Make sure your attire is business appropriate. Don't come in dressed in something loud. Wear something conservative and of good quality, but look sharp. A nice red tie or a colorful dress is fine, but stick to business suits when possible.

Don't try to express your uniqueness via your choice of clothing. I've seen a woman come into an interview dressed well but carrying a pocketbook that was given to her by her great-grandmother and is now falling apart. Grandma would want you to get this job; she'd be okay with it if you left the purse at home during your interview.

Have nice, clean-looking materials. Carry your résumé in a simple, tasteful folder when you come to your interview. Bring a nice pen. You don't want to walk in the door looking disorganized, or pull your résumé out of a laptop case and risk a ton of papers falling on the floor. Don't fold your résumé and put it inside your pocketbook or coat pocket. It gets wrinkled and sloppy.

People want to get to know you, so during the interview, you may be asked questions about your interests, hobbies, and family. Make sure you're prepared to answer such questions. I've witnessed people, when such questions arise, become absolutely too casual and relaxed. They go off on a tangent, talking about things that are not pertinent to the interview. So have a statement ready.

Some of the top managers in the world have varied interests outside of work. They're accomplished in areas such as music or sports. Some managers I've known have been expert violinists and great guitarists. You want to be able to talk about what you're great at and what you enjoy in a way that's clear, concise, professional, and focused. And if the manager continues the conversation, go with it. If not, just return to the point you were at in the REAPRICH process.

Managers are really looking to see if you have excellence in other areas of your life. Those are the questions behind the questions. For example, they may ask, "What would your best friend say about you? What three words would he or she use to describe you?" That's a question I often use, because it catches people off guard. But not you: you'll be ready.

Sometimes I'll ask, "Tell me about integrity. What does that word mean to you?" Or I'll look at people and say, "Who are you?" Even though the questions are intensely personal, never drop your professional demeanor. Mine your REAPRICH preparation for answers that will put your attributes in the best possible light.

One thing that happens all too often is that people with great backgrounds, people who should be shoo-in candidates for a position, lose out because they were negative about a prior job or bad-mouthed their current employer. You should never say something like, "The reason I'm looking for a new job is I can't stand the company I'm with now." Or, "My boss is an idiot."

You can ruin your chances with a negative statement. After all, if you'll speak badly about your current employer, it makes hiring managers suspect you'll do the same about their company. If they sense that negativity, they'll probe for it, so make sure nothing you say puts a negative focus on a company you've been with or the one you're currently working for. And understand: truth is no defense here. If you're asked about a job where you had a truly awful experience, you simply say, "The company was going through some changes and I saw that their success probably wouldn't be as robust as I had initially hoped. I have some very strong goals for my career. I'd like to be able to carry them out at your company. I've done some research; I feel it's a great company and here's why …"

Likewise, if a manager asks, "Why do you want to be with our company?" he or she wants you to give an intelligent response. You can't just say, "Oh, it's the best in the world," and hope to impress anyone. Managers *may* want to know that you've interviewed at other places, which indicates you're in demand and discerning. But leave this to them. Only address

INSIDER SECRET #10:
Many hiring managers like to disqualify candidates based on commonsense errors because it gives them a definitive reason for saying no and not taking a risk. Managers also think that a candidate who's lacking common sense is not detail-oriented or intelligent, or that they simply don't care.

other companies if they ask where else you're interviewing. They may also ask why you like that company, why you don't, or how it stacks up to their own. They want to know that you've done some research, that you're not just someone who settles for the first thing that comes along. Discussing other firms you've interviewed with is another area where you want to keep it positive, even if the manager seems to be prompting you to say something negative about the competition. You can never go wrong taking the high road.

Being on time is another way to show you have respect for the company, the position, and the hiring manager's time. Remember that being "on time" for an interview really means "at least ten minutes early," so that you have time to relax, focus, and check your appearance in a mirror.

Some executive positions have a rather lengthy, multistage interview process. By the time you're on your fourth or fifth interview, you will have built great rapport with the manager or vice president. Don't let that sense of familiarity lead you to drop your professional demeanor. By all means, smile and always be engaged, energetic, and positive, but don't let down your professionalism—ever. You can open up a bit more than you might on a first or second interview, to create a deeper connection, but always remember you are in the leader's office.

COMMONSENSE RECAP WORKSHEET

1. Name three good practices that you should always consider when going for an interview.

2. Write down a response to the question, "What are your interests and hobbies outside of work?" Practice it. Remember to keep it brief, and don't go off on a tangent.

3. Write down a response to the question, "What three words would your best friend use to describe you?" Briefly explain why those adjectives apply to you, tying them into how these qualities make you a good candidate.

CHAPTER 11
YOU'VE GOT THE JOB ... NOW WHAT?
BEING AN ENLIGHTENED EMPLOYEE

"The most thought-provoking thing in our
thought-provoking time is that we are still not thinking."
—MARTIN HEIDEGGER

There are many enlightened business leaders who work every day toward living lives of integrity. If you can get close to one of them, you'll have a better career. If you can *become* one of them, you may change the course of history.

If you work toward making a difference for others while learning to manage your inner state, you'll have peace and happiness beyond any paycheck. Helping others leads to an inner sense of reward. As Kahlil Gibran said in his book *The Prophet*, "Work is love made visible."

If you can do something you're passionate about, your chances of success and of sustaining your enthusiasm for your work will be much higher. Your sense of caring and commitment will also shine through more easily. Whether or not you're working your dream job, certain practices in both your personal and professional lives will enhance not just your job performance, but your sense of fulfillment and overall well-being.

First, if you want to be elite and rise up through the ranks, you have to adopt a code of integrity.

Part of that means keeping personal information private. Unfortunately, in corporate America today, you don't want to be an open book. Never tell anyone something you don't want everyone else to know. Some people thrive on gossip and other people's drama. Don't tell people about your health problems, family problems, love life, or personal mishaps. Save those for your personal relationships.

INSIDER SECRET #11:
Managers like employees who can bring both excitement and balance to the company.

Another part of integrity is avoiding gossip. That's something that many people find difficult. The fact is, people like to talk. If you're in an interview, and you know someone in common with the interviewer, you may be asked, "How did you like interviewing with so and so?" Never, ever make a negative comment about someone else. Things you say can get back to the wrong people and derail your chances.

Gossip, one way or another, will almost always come back to haunt you. It could be three months or ten years in the future. Someone who's not a coworker today could, somewhere down the road, be a critical part of your team, a partner, or even your boss. If that person thinks you've said something cruel about them, it will come back to bite you.

Remember that code of integrity? Think of it as being the *"Book of 1,000 Secrets."*

I know a man who is an absolute open book. He's phenomenal at what he does, except anytime something goes off track, he tells five or ten people about it. He tells customers about what went wrong, why the company isn't treating him well, or just how messed up things are. Not surprisingly, although he's very skilled at his job, he's never been promoted. It's not the first time I've seen this inability to filter oneself inhibit someone's career growth.

Finding a mentor you can trust and understand is a critical piece of avoiding these pitfalls. Some people pay personal coaches just to review their business interactions or to talk about a highly difficult employee or manager. Difficulties with coworkers, miscommunications, missed deadlines, and projects gone wrong are all opportunities for growth if understood and explored properly.

MANEUVERING INTERNALLY, RISING THROUGH THE RANKS, AND GETTING PROMOTED

Once you have the job, it's important to know how to navigate the corporate culture to continue to grow in your position. One of the key ways is to find someone who needs something done. Often this involves going outside of your job description. If you want to grow or get promoted into a different department, look for ways to be useful to the people in that department. Show the manager you are worthy of being on that team. Call him up, or send an email about something that will let him know you've taken an interest in his needs. For instance, has the manager published an article on the company website, or sent out a memo? Email him your thoughts. Give freely of your time, even if it adds a few extra hours to your workweek. If it's eventually going to raise your salary twenty or forty or sixty thousand dollars, isn't it worth the investment?

This works not only when you're already employed by a company, but when you're trying to get into it as well. For instance, if you're just coming out of school and want to get into a certain field, pursuing an unpaid internship is one way to be of service and show off your skills to potential hirers.

Some people swear by going to graduate school, and it can be wonderful. However, an advanced degree is not an automatic ticket to success, and in some disciplines it may be completely superfluous. You may just need to focus on upping your game, going above and beyond, and becoming excellent in your current position so that your higher-ups will see you as an employee who brings added value to the job, no matter what.

Another way to go above and beyond is to read an article by

someone who's an expert in a field, then send an email and ask if you can interview that person for a half hour. Take the person to lunch. Impress him or her by asking intelligent, cogent questions. People love it when someone asks about what they've done and how they've done it. Everybody likes to be recognized for what they've accomplished.

Be persistent—but not obnoxious. I've mentioned how the person who gave me my first opportunity was someone I called almost daily for about six months. I built a relationship and got to know him. It was the most unlikely of chances—this was one of the most elite companies in the world—but he did give me a shot.

If you're lucky enough to have someone give you that kind of a chance, rise to the occasion. If you say you're going to do something—you're going to call, you're going to arrive at a certain time—then do it. If you're asked to research something and get it back with answers in three days, don't take six. In fact, get it back in two.

PRACTICES, PRACTICES, PRACTICES!

Practices are not only instrumental to preparing yourself for an interview, but once you're in your dream job, they become even more critical. By practices, I mean living up to your word. Saying, "I'm going to do this by this date." Or, "I commit to being there at this time."

If you absolutely need to extend a deadline or change a commitment, call the person who's expecting the work and renegotiate, then recommit to the new plan. This requires you to call *before* the deadline and say, "I haven't finished this, and here's why. But I know I made a commitment to you by this date. Here's what I propose we do from here ..." Most often, the person to whom you've made the commitment will be reassured of both your integrity you're your ability to do the job, because you've addressed the situation head-on and proposed a solution. On the other hand, if that person doesn't hear from you or see you, he or she will wonder if you've forgotten about it.

I once heard renowned psychologist M. Scott Peck say that the biggest plague in the world is human laziness. I see people who say, "I want to do this. I want to get this job." Yet they never take time to prepare their résumé, project a sense of urgency, or take the immediate action that's needed to move forward. Yes, all of this does take energy. It takes initiative. But if you want to get the job, keep the job, and advance in the job, you need to bring your energy and your A-game every day of the week. The rewards are there for the taking.

BEING AN ENLIGHTENED EMPLOYEE WORKSHEET

Take a few minutes to reflect on past work experiences and respond to the following:

1. Jot down an example of a time when you felt someone went too far in sharing their personal life in a work setting. How do you think this may have affected their professional life?

2. Is there now or has there ever been a time in which you could have gone above and beyond the call of duty to help a coworker or otherwise make yourself useful outside of your normal purview of responsibilities? What could you have done? What stopped you from taking that step?

CHAPTER 12

CHANGING CAREERS AND ADVICE FOR NEW GRADUATES

"Go to the edge of the cliff and jump off.
Build your wings on the way down."
—Ray Bradbury

If you're changing careers, it's once again critically important to communicate your successes or winning areas on your résumé. Show potential employers that you have already been a success in your current career. If they see this success, they'll feel more at ease in taking a risk on you, even though you have no experience in their field. The trick is to initially align any existing skills that overlap your new career and highlight them.

You must also spend time finding out who you want to work for in your new industry. Not all organizations or managers are created equal. Do your research to discover which firms or individuals in your target industry are doing great things, then concentrate your efforts on those firms and individuals. Finding an article that a potential employer has written or another sincere way to congratulate them on something they've accomplished is a good way to open up a dialogue. You also want to use anyone you might know who could get you in front of them.

Remember too, that busy people's time is short and therefore valuable. Don't be resentful if it takes you ten tries to see someone. Never get upset, just work hard and keep making overtures. And think outside the box: don't be afraid to go to extremes and send something noticeable to get someone's attention or thank them. Learning Annex founder Bill Zanker talks about how he has often sent flowers to get a business prospect to simply pay attention to his offer or proposal. When interviewing for a corporate job you need to respect professional boundaries, so finding something that conveys thoughtfulness or creativity is often the best way to go. You could call someone like an administrative assistant or receptionist to figure out the interviewer's favorite food or color—anything that will get you noticed. Sending a nice handwritten note is often a great gesture and can show personal thought and creativity.

It's also critical to offer your time as a volunteer in your new field, preferably on a regular basis. Volunteering free time, even if it's just five hours a week, is a great way to get people to know you, see your work ethic, and have a direct experience of what it's like working with you, which means you won't be starting out cold. Employers also appreciate the initiative this shows, as it means you'll work hard once you begin a job with them.

Another tactic is to leave power voicemails or send letters to targeted people outlining your results and desire to move into their field. **A power voicemail is one that differentiates you by stating your results, compliments the target about theirs, then asks for a meeting to discuss their accomplishments.** This is less intrusive and even allows you to let them know that you want to "interview" them to learn from their great expertise.

A power voicemail to someone within your industry might sound something like, "Fred, this is John Chase. I've been the top salesperson at EdjTronix for five years, with 130 percent of quota, winning two number-one ranking awards, and I had the highest customer satisfaction three years in a row. I'd like to explore an opportunity in your organization, as I believe it's the next step on my career path. Please call me at (phone number)." If you were trying for a position in an industry where you have no current experience, it might sound more like this: "Fred, this is John Chase, I noticed you're a top engineering leader and I've been top 10 percent in the research science industry and did four specializations on chemical plastics research after getting a 3.9 GPA and two awards in college. I'd like to interview for an associate engineer position with your company. I also researched your top two published papers and loved the part about flow control processes. I wonder if I could take you to coffee next week to discuss your work? Please call me at (phone number)."

INSIDER SECRET #12:
You can get people's attention and create value for them and yourself. But to do so, you must leave your comfort zone and take risks.

You also may want to send a handwritten note that aligns with the facts in your voice message. Even then, you may still have to call two or three times before you get a meeting. Persistence pays off. This is the kind of thing I was referring to when I mentioned going outside the box and leaving your comfort zone. None of it will feel natural at first—that's okay. The only thing that matters is how it's received at the other end.

I've hired people who had 75 percent of the experience and knowledge I needed over people who had 100 percent. Why? Because I could see that they were hungry, motivated, and they were ready to do whatever it took to succeed.

If you're a new graduate, you need to capitalize on whatever you've achieved so far, whether it was getting a high grade point average or having been a top 5 percent varsity sports player or a leader in student government. Mention any awards you've won, even if it was Employee of the Month at Dairy Queen or Staples. Were you promoted to shift supervisor at your summer job? That's a result you should be highlighting. Show that you excel or make an impact of some sort in every aspect of your life, or that you somehow do some things better, faster, or more reliably than your peers.

Asking for information-only interviews or going to a location where a person you want to work for is giving a speech or workshop is also another way to begin a relationship. It's also an effective tactic to develop a relationship with that person's secretary or gatekeeper, as he or she often knows more about the person you want face time with than anyone else. Polite persistence is the key to getting this time.

You can also find out if someone you want to work with has special interests—sports, hobbies, charities, or service clubs—and begin getting involved in some of those. As a last resort, you can send something to get yourself noticed, like flowers, food, wine, beer, a picture, card, or tickets to an event. Keep in mind that there's a limit on the worth of gifts that can be accepted by some corporate employees and executives which is usually in the neighborhood of one hundred dollars.

While I was recruiting for Oracle, a man three years out of school once sent me a laminated overview of key points about why he would be the best choice for an inside sales job at the company. The envelope had candy in it! That was unexpected, and it got my attention. I told the hiring manager about it but warned him that the man's résumé wasn't as strong as some others we had.

The manager responded, "If he did that, I want to see him anyway." The manager noticed and appreciated the extra effort.

Remember: whether you're just starting out or trying to make a mid-course correction to your career, never believe that you can't succeed beyond your wildest dreams. Work hard, have principles, and make sure you live according to your word. In a short time, you can be further than you ever dreamed.

By the way … the guy with the candy? He got the job!

CHANGING CAREERS WORKSHEET

1. List a few opportunities for volunteer work in your area that you would be interested in doing. Want to take it one step further? Sign up and volunteer!

2. Write the script for a power voicemail you could send someone in your field or that you might send to someone in a field you are interested in breaking into. Record yourself and listen as though you are the potential employer.

CHAPTER 13
POWER RÉSUMÉ WRITING

"How many people live on the reputation of the reputation they might have made!"
—Oliver Wendell Holmes

Your résumé is a portrait of you, a picture painted in words. But an article published in March 2012 entitled "What Your Resume Is Up Against" by Susan Adams for Forbes.com reports that recruiters spend an average of just 6.25 seconds looking at a candidate's résumé before deciding whether he or she is a fit for a job. That means your résumé has to be more than a work of art; it has to be a precision tool, laser-focused on getting a manager's attention.

INSIDER SECRET #13: Recruiters and hiring managers probably won't read every word of your résumé. You have just seconds to get their attention, make an impression, and get an interview.

How do you do that? Make sure the most compelling things about you are placed where they'll get noticed.

On your résumé, the first two to four bullets under each entry—each position you've held or company you've worked for—should speak to your *results*. The next two bullets should speak to your *process* and your *relationships*. Remember: these three elements—results, process, and relationships—are the ones that do the heavy lifting during the interview itself. Doesn't it make sense to put them at center stage on your résumé?

Let's say you worked for a large electronics firm. The following are examples of the kind of information that should be included in the first two to six bullets under that listing:

- Received top-level performance ratings every year. Completed all projects 10 percent ahead of time and 15 percent under budget
- Ranked number one account manager in the Northeast for the full year, 2007, 2006, 2005
- Ranked in top 5 percent of achievement
- Won the largest number of new accounts companywide, 2004–2006
- Top engineer
- Top 1 percent recognitions for my contribution to research
- Won Employee of the Month, fall of 2007

The next two bullets under this job listing should deal with your process and your relationships:

- Logged 20 percent more research hours than anyone in the department (Process)
- Personally mentored by Alton Haines, senior vice president of engineering (Relationships)

Now you've put the critical components of your résumé where they're most likely to be seen and noticed, and you've done it in a way that takes just seconds to read and absorb. People don't want long stories. When I see a résumé with long stories but no results, I know that candidate is trying to pull the wool over my eyes. (To be fair, maybe they're just uneducated in the REAPRICH method.) Any good recruiter or good manager will spot fluff and filler on a résumé.

So, either you have results or you have to get them. If you don't have specific results or ways to show how you've differentiated yourself, you really need to stop at this point in your career and ask why. Why have I not put more time in? Why have I not differentiated myself? If you want to move up the ranks, if you want to be elite, just doing what's expected won't get you there. I'm not suggesting you have to work eighty hours a week and burn out. I am suggesting that you have to put in whatever time it takes to create a "wow factor."

Once you have that "wow factor," make sure it's front and center. For instance, people always seem to put awards at the bottom of their résumés. What a huge mistake! Managers want to see your awards under each company listing. Some people leave it off altogether! They say, "Oh, I feel like I'm being arrogant if I put my awards on there." No, no, no. You're seeking a job, competing with anywhere from a hundred and fifty to ten thousand other people. You must be willing to show how you are different, better, and accomplished!

Many job seekers ask me whether it's absolutely essential to include an objective. If you're early in your career or changing jobs, an objective near the top of your résumé will help people understand what you're looking for. (See next page for experience examples from a power résumé.)

Some people lead with education, possibly because of the mistaken notion that things should be listed chronologically on a résumé. I say your educational background should only be put in a place of prominence if you have an advanced degree with honors or are applying for a position within academia. Otherwise, put it at the bottom where it can be found by those who want a deeper look into your background but won't deflect attention away from important current achievements.

Sample Résumé Format

Rachel Simmonds
2433 Success Summit Road
Talent, OR 97540
541-124-7228
rsimmonds@serviceprovider.com

Education:

Haas School of Business, UC Berkeley; Berkeley, CA, June 2001
MBA International Business Development, **Honors, 3.7 GPA, 15th out of 112**

University of Massachusetts, Boston, MA, June 1998
BA Business Administration/Marketing

Summary:

Top 1% award-winning executive with continuous experience marketing and branding products for domestic and international markets. Won 3 marketing awards including national magazine recognition, securing over 100 new relationships, and bringing in 85% of assignments ahead of goal. Deep C-level connections internationally in B-to-B and B-to-C Tier 1–3 companies.

Experience:

2010–15 Earth Built Building Products, Inc., Anaheim, CA, Director of Marketing
- *Increased US market penetration from 12% to 67% in two years*
- *Secured 21 new distributors* to open new markets in Australia, Norway, Denmark, Sweden, and Mexico
- *Awarded Marketer of the Year* from *Builder+Architect* **magazine, 2012**
- Responsible for building relationships with major architectural and engineering firms, Fortune 500 construction companies, and international accounts

2004–10 Bass & Treble Sound Labs, Portland, OR, Director of Marketing
- *Winner of two Clio Awards (2009).* Consumer product *sales increased 72%* after consumer ad campaign launch
- *Recruited by company CEO and founder. Mentored 3 people into leadership*
- *Secured 22 new OEM relationships* for car audio division including *Acura* and *Harley-Davidson.*
- *Started marine division* and secured OEM relationship with *Sunseeker Yachts*
- Responsible for national *"Feel the Sound"* consumer ad campaign
- Strengthened consumer brand awareness by establishing a presence at local and regional consumer "enthusiast" shows. Created an infrastructure among retail dealer base to provide show booth staffing and demo models in exchange for wholesale discounts, terms, and incentives

2001–04 Owl's Nest Winery, Willamette, OR, Director of Advertising
- *Made Owl's Nest label the #1 recognized brand* of Oregon wine among consumers (*Oregonian* reader poll 2004)
- *Promoted in 5 months* from entry-level copywriter position to *Director of Advertising*
- *Brought in 12 assignments* ahead of goal
- *Designed and implemented* the winery's first consumer ad campaign
- *Attracted and retained a Michelin-rated chef* and restaurateur as technical advisor to the winemaker. Currently serve as comembers of Feed the Nation Foundation advisory board
- Consulted with owner and winemakers on varietal production year to year based on consumer trend research

References furnished upon request

POWER RÉSUMÉ WORKSHEET

1. Jot down some ideas for enhancements you could make on your own résumé based on what you've learned. Remember, first highlight three results, then process, and finally relationships.

2. Now that you've brainstormed some ideas, go update your résumé!

CHAPTER 14
TOUGH QUESTIONS AND HOW TO ANSWER THEM

"Be Prepared."
—Robert Baden-Powell
(official Boy Scout motto)

While I don't recommend memorizing answers to anticipated interview questions, there are a few common ones managers like to ask because they tend to take candidates by surprise. You'll note in the following examples that many answers are mined from your REAPRICH preparation, which serves a dual purpose: presenting a cohesive message to the interviewer by reinforcing your main points, and giving you less to memorize. Both are confidence boosters.

Who are you? Incorporate three personal and three or four professional positives into your answer. For example, "I'm an extremely hard worker who loves to finish before deadline and win awards. But I also put just as much emphasis on being a great dad and husband. I enjoy waterskiing, mountain climbing, and playing guitar, and have recently gotten into the power of great nutrition."

Why should I hire you? Use four positives from your results list and two from your process and relationships lists. Keep it to about a minute.

Give an example of a time you tried your best and failed. You need to be honest here. Describe the goal, what went wrong, and how you approached it. Most important, end with what you did to remedy the situation, and *what you learned* from it.

Who was the worst boss (or employee) you ever worked with? Remember the prohibition on badmouthing? Even if you had an awful boss or coworker, it is not good to get into negatives or specifics like incompetence. Instead, describe this person as someone who challenged you beyond what you thought you could handle. Then show that the experience taught you tolerance, patience, and how to act professionally under all circumstances.

What four words would someone close to you use to describe you? This is one I use frequently. Often it throws people for a loop. If you can't describe yourself as others see you in a positive way, it may mean that no one sees you positively. Be prepared for this one and don't even hesitate with your answer. It could make someone question your ability to build relationships.

Who was your best mentor? Hopefully, you have someone on your relationships list who falls into the category of mentor. Be quick with your answer here too. If you can't describe someone's positive effect on you, then people might question whether you can build relationships, accept authority, learn from others, and collaborate.

What do you feel you will bring to this organization? Once again, mine your REAPRICH lists. Make a statement that highlights four or five items from your results list, two from process, and three from relationships.

Where do you want to be in five years? Don't say you want the manager's job. Let's face it—self-protection is a human trait shared by even the best managers. A good manager will appreciate your ambition; a mediocre or bad one may feel threatened. Instead say, "I want to progress in the organization and be one of the fastest-learning and -growing employees. I'd also like to be of maximum use to you as *you* rise up the ladder."

INSIDER SECRET #14:
If you follow the REAPRICH method, you'll answer most of your interviewer's questions before they're asked.

What is your greatest weakness? Don't simply turn a negative into a positive. That's an outdated approach that could come across as a lack of creativity. Instead, think of an honest negative that's something that won't count you out of a job. "I've realized I expect more from people than they expect from themselves," is one example. Another is, "I need to learn to step back and look at the big picture more often, as I am used to driving things quickly." Or, "I don't enjoy details so although I'm careful to keep track of them, I always partner myself with someone I know will catch all the details while I'm moving at light speed."

What is your ninety-day plan to be successful here? Before the interview, think about whether there's a way to come up with an intelligent plan based on what you've learned through your research of the company and the position. If not, come prepared to talk about one from a past opportunity. At least you'll demonstrate that you're a planner who's always ready.

Give me an example of where you took a difficult customer or situation and turned it into a win. Everyone has success stories of this kind. Pick one and boil the details down into a concise, punchy response.

TOUGH QUESTIONS WORKSHEET

Answer the questions reviewed in this chapter as if you were in an interview:

1. Who are you?

2. Why should I hire you?

3. Give an example of a time you tried your best and failed.

4. Who was the worst boss (or employee) you ever worked with?

5. What four words would someone close to you use to describe you?

6. Who was your best mentor?

7. What do you feel you will bring to this organization?

8. Where do you want to be in five years?

9. What is your greatest weakness?

10. What is your ninety-day plan to be successful here?

11. Give me an example of where you took a difficult customer or situation and turned it into a win.

CHAPTER 15
WINNING STRATEGIES TO BE A HEALTHY, ENERGIZED, AND WELL-ROUNDED EXECUTIVE OR EMPLOYEE

"Champions aren't made in gyms, champions are made from something they have deep inside them—a desire, a dream, a vision ... They have to have the skill and the will. But the will must be stronger than the skill."
—MUHAMMAD ALI

If you follow the principles in this book from beginning to end, you'll have the opportunity to succeed and a tremendous edge over those with whom you'll be competing. There's one other element that will affect your chances, and that's your inner landscape: character, spirituality, drive, balance, and health—both physical and mental.

You may think these things are set in stone, but in fact they're malleable as gold. Throughout our lives we're constantly changing in response to changes around us. Usually, those changes are unconscious. I'm simply suggesting you take an honest look at that landscape and make *conscious* changes, trusting to your innate human attraction to the positive.

Develop a sense of urgency. Don't have one? Get one. One of my top early mentors at Oracle used to stress a sense of urgency in defining and driving the beginnings and actualizations of success. If you don't have it, people will leave you behind and none of your results will get recognized. Just so you know that I practice what I preach, I'm writing this at 4:30 in the morning. Why? I felt the need to get out of my normal comfort zone.

Practice stress reduction. Many top executives practice stress reduction, and I don't mean through partying or even exercise. Exercise can be wonderful, but today many top executives are practicing things like meditation, visualization, or prayer as a way of grounding themselves and calming down. I can't overstate the effectiveness of practices like these. There's a kind of energy available to everyone who goes beyond synthetic knowledge to find inner peace. This energy can help guide you in your daily choices and provide clarity. I meditate and pray every morning. It gives me clarity and peace for my day.

"Ah, but I'm not a religious person," you say. You don't have to be religious to pray. You don't have to pray to anyone or anything specific. Just say, "Hey, if there's something out there, I need some calming today. Please bring some energy in to help me." Developing a daily meditation practice is another great stress reducer. Meditation is believed to lower blood pressure and heart rate, as well as boost the immune system. Information about many of the most popular and effective meditation practices is readily available online. These practices include Insight Meditation (InsightMeditation.org), Ananda Sangha (Ananda.org), and Self-Realization Fellowship (Yogananda-SRF.org). If you want to learn about the most highly regarded, deeply effective airplane route in mediation and yoga, refer to chapter 26 in *The Spiritual*

> **INSIDER SECRET #15:**
> The powers and energy that lie outside our synthetic knowledge are groundbreaking vehicles for change.

Science of Kriya Yoga by Goswami Kriyananda.

Read these great books to help you relax personally and grow professionally:

- *Real Magic* or *The Awakened Life* by Dr. Wayne W. Dyer
- *Care of the Soul: A Guide for Cultivating Depth and Sacredness in Everyday Life* by Thomas Moore
- *Awaken the Giant Within* and *Unlimited Power* by Tony Robbins
- *A Return to Love: Reflections on the Principles of "A Course in Miracles"* by Marianne Williamson
- *The Road Less Traveled* or *The Different Drum* by M. Scott Peck
- *Mindset: The New Psychology of Success* by Carol Dweck

Invite all of these sources into your process. If you want to be the best version of yourself, listen to great speakers in all areas of professional and personal growth, and also read great writers. This is all part of making you a well-rounded person and job candidate.

Give yourself a fitness and nutrition check-up. If you don't have a fitness program and eat healthy foods, you're missing out on a way to increase both your energy and your mental acuity. Not to mention that employers like fit people. They're less of a risk and a liability, so being fit increases your chances of being hired and being promoted. Create quiet time to recharge and be creative. This time when you can sit and relax is important, but you have to create it for yourself. Make it a priority because it won't happen on its own. Carve out at least ten minutes during your workday to unplug and unwind, whether it's reading the sports page with a cup of tea or taking a walk around the block. On weekends, indulge in activities that stimulate the creative centers of your brain. If you paint, draw, sew, write, or play music, great! If not, consider taking up a creative pastime or sign up for a class that will nurture that side of you. Such activities can create a state known as "flow," where time seems to stand still, resulting in a deep sense of calm and well-being.

Learn to visualize the results you want. All the best books written about success have a common factor: people often become what they think about. Ever think about someone you haven't seen in a while, and that person suddenly appears? Dreams and goals that seem out of reach can become real through your continuous manifestation of the invisible mind and soul.

Starting five days before your interview, take five minutes a day of quiet time, alone, and picture positive things happening. Picture the outcome you want. Visualize what you want to accomplish. Visualize people saying, "Wow, that was great!" Visualize yourself winning. It's amazing what a powerful vehicle the mind is.

When people fail, I often ask them if they visualized that outcome. They say, "Yes, with a lot of fear wrapped around it." Dr. Wayne Dyer, one of the world's most successful and inspirational motivational speakers, said, "We become what we think about all day long." So if you focus on negative things—on failing at a job, on your fears about why you can't do something, that you'll never win—guess what? That fear, negativity, and worry will show up in the physical world. To work successfully, your visualizations should be around good intentions. By the way, Dyer's *Real Magic* is a must-read book. I also love his audio series, *The Awakened Life*. I listened to it many years ago during a time of major change and personal upheaval and it was life-changing.

Conquer your fear. To be great in an interview, you need to overcome fear. That doesn't mean you never experience fear; quite the contrary. We all feel fear. Conquering it means standing in the middle of fear, allowing yourself to experience feeling it and *not* being paralyzed by it. Meditation and breathing exercises along with prayer and taking care of yourself through exercise and nutrition are very important.

Here's an exercise to help you get the upper hand on your fear. First, write it down. Be specific. Don't just say, "I'm afraid of having a bad interview." Dig a little deeper to find out what it is you're really scared of. "I'm afraid I'll freeze up and forget to say something important." Or, "I'm afraid the interviewer will judge me for not finishing college." Then answer the following questions about your fear, in writing:

- When do I first remember experiencing this fear?
- What is a recent example of this fear in my life? How did I react to the fear?
- How did others react to my reaction?
- What kinds of circumstances were set in motion by my fear?
- What should I have done instead?
- What is a good affirmation or prayer about eliminating this fear?

When you've finished, read your answers to another person you trust. If you there's no one available, read them alone. Either way, read them aloud, and allow yourself to release the fear with your words. This is an important step because fear thrives in darkness. Once you've let in the light by speaking your fears aloud, you'll feel them diminish.

Motivate yourself to follow through. People tend to think of motivation as something outside themselves, something that either comes or doesn't, but in fact motivation is most often a matter of commitment. Hesitating to make commitments can become habitual, and that can be dangerous. It means you've got a good chance of staying stuck wherever you are right now. People often wait for motivation, or to "feel like it" before they move forward. Regardless of how you feel, you must get out of bed and take action.

Self-esteem is partially developed from the repeated experience of meeting commitments head-on and coming through on those commitments on time, or even ahead of time.

Start by learning to make and keep commitments to yourself. Every day, write down the actions you are going to take the next day, and on each step of your journey. In order to reach maximum effectiveness, you need to begin to work toward a 100 percent hit rate on that to-do list. When you're consistently reaching 100 percent, up it to 120 percent. Getting to 120 percent means that you did more than your daily goal, that you overachieved. In the beginning, living up to your commitments is like learning to ride a bike, or using a part of your body again after a serious injury. It's awkward at first, but it gets easier the more you do it.

Don't be the drunk at the party! Green tea or chamomile tea is a much healthier relaxation tool than alcohol. Alcohol can reduce levels of serotonin, the "well-being hormone," and increase cortisol, the "stress hormone," sending you into a downward spiral. Stress also reduces serotonin, so stress and alcohol together can make you feel like a shell of the person you are. If you're playing too hard, you have to make time to recharge.

There's another reason to limit your alcohol consumption: drinking around work colleagues, especially drinking to excess, will negatively affect your reputation at work. I remember an Oracle corporate function where a newly hired Oracle sales employee was sitting next to the executive VP of sales. He was trying to build rapport, and doing well for quite a while … until he threw up on the bar. All the progress he'd made vanished in that instant. I also saw a Harvard grad who'd played rugby start head-butting everyone at a similar event after a lot of drinks. And then there was the female manager who was circumspect and professional during working hours, but had a habit of getting very drunk at after-hours company events and telling people what she *really* thought. Keep it together.

You never want to be the gossip *du jour* around the watercooler. (Unless it's for your stellar achievements and meteoric rise to the top!) If you're having alcohol or drug problems, please look into the twelve-step programs offered by Alcoholics Anonymous (AA) or Narcotics Anonymous (NA). Many famous people and business leaders are leading happy lives of continuous sobriety thanks to these programs. If you're a spiritual person, ask for help through prayer. Then go get the appropriate professional help. Those who ask for that help are the strong ones. They often become society's future winners.

Adjust your outlook. I've seen people begin to make huge accomplishments by putting in a huge amount of effort, but first, they had to decide to put in that effort. It started with an outlook, a willingness to go above and beyond with tenacity. The universe may test your commitment to hard work and willingness to go outside the box and do different and creative things. My own commitment has been tested many times, but I've found that when I am highly responsible, take care of details, make that last phone call, and manage my internal well-being, I get results.

It's also important to recognize the people in your life who don't support you in winning. Learn not to listen to them. Consider taking a little time away from them—or a lot!—when you're focusing on overachievement.

Create a platform or space for excellence through due diligence. Doing things like paying bills, returning phone calls, or finishing tasks you've left incomplete clears physical and mental clutter while it wipes your karmic slate clean. If you can get the energy of the universe behind you through proper action, you'll have a very good chance to accomplish expectations beyond your wildest dreams.

I've crossed off everything on two dream lists I made for myself earlier in life and am in the process of writing a third. The rewards are the peace that comes with having continuous employment, a satisfying career, the ability to be with family, and the opportunity to give back to others. The mission of this book is to give the same chance to all those people I've seen miss out on these rewards because they weren't prepared. Gandhi said, "Be the difference you wish to see in the world ..." It's my hope that reading this book will make a real difference in your career path, and your path through life.

I wish you energy, excellence, and success.